Belair Early Years Number & Calculating

Cherri Moseley

Acknowledgements

The author and publishers would like to thank the headteacher, staff and children of Bignold First School and Nursery for their invaluable help in the production of this book.

The author would like to say a special 'thank you' to Emily Beck, Jill Lamb, Jas Ryan and their Foundation Stage Team for their support and to Mel Clarke for her creativity. She would also like to thank Harry Marsh and Gatsby for starting the ball rolling that led to this book.

Ladybird Sixes (page 29)

Published by Collins, An imprint of HarperCollins*Publishers*
77 – 85 Fulham Palace Road, Hammersmith, London, W6 8JB

Browse the complete Collins catalogue at
www.collinseducation.com

© HarperCollins*Publishers* Limited 2012
Previously published in 2007 by Folens
First published in 2004 by Belair Publications

10 9 8 7 6 5 4 3

ISBN-13 978-0-00-744800-5

Cherri Moseley asserts her moral rights to be identified as the author of this work

British Library Cataloguing in Publication Data
A Catalogue record for this publication is available from the British Library

All Early learning goals, Areas of learning and development, and Aspects of learning quoted in this book are taken from the *Statutory Framework for the Early Years Foundation Stage*, Department for Education, 2012 (available at www.education.gov.uk/publications). This information is licensed under the terms of the Open Government Licence (www.nationalarchives.gov.uk/doc/open-government-licence).

Every effort has been made to trace copyright holders and to obtain their permission for the use of copyright material. The authors and publishers will gladly receive any information enabling them to rectify any error or omission in subsequent editions.

Cover concept: Mount Deluxe   Cover design: Linda Miles, Lodestone Publishing
Cover photography: Nigel Meager   Commissioning editor: Zöe Nichols
Editor: Jennifer Steele   Page layout: Philippa Jarvis
Illustrations: Sara Silcock   Photography: GGS Photo Graphics Limited/Kelvin Freeman

Photographs: p39 Woman Handling Python Boy Stroking Snake © TRIP/D MCGILL; p42 Girl Looking in Pumpkin ©TRIP/H ROGERS Publications; p21 'Ten White Snowmen' © John Foster, from *A Blue Poetry Paintbox* (Oxford University Press), included by permission of author; p32 *How Many Snails?* By Paul Giganti, Jr (HarperCollins), reproduced by permission of HarperCollins; p40 *Ten Seeds* by Ruth Brown (Andersen Press), reproduced by permission of Andersen Press; p56 *The Doorbell Rang* by Pat Hutchins (Scholastic), reproduced by permission of Scholastic.

Printed and bound by Rotolito Lombarda S.p.A. - Italy

Contents

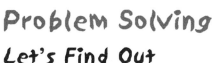

Introduction

The **Belair Early Years** series has been well-loved by early years educators working with the under-fives for many years. This re-launched edition of these practical resource books offers popular, tried and tested ideas, all written by professionals working in early years education. The inspirational ideas will support educators in delivering the three characteristics of effective teaching and learning identified in the Statutory Framework for the Early Years Foundation Stage 2012: playing and exploring, active learning, and creating and thinking critically.

The guiding principles at the heart of the EYFS Framework 2012 emphasise the importance of the unique child, the impact of positive relationships and enabling environments on children's learning and development, and that children develop and learn in different ways and at different rates. The 'hands on' activities in **Belair Early Years** fit this ethos perfectly and are ideal for developing the EYFS prime areas of learning (Communication and language, Physical development, Personal, social and emotional development) and specific areas of learning (Literacy, Mathematics, Understanding the world, Expressive arts and design) which should be implemented through a mix of child-initiated and adult-led activities. Purposeful play is vital for children's development, whether leading their own play or participating in play guided by adults. Where appropriate, suggestions for Free Play opportunities are identified.

Throughout this book full-colour photography is used to offer inspiration for presenting and developing children's individual work with creative display ideas for each theme. Display is highly beneficial as a stimulus for further exploration, as well as providing a visual communication of ideas and a creative record of children's learning journeys. In addition to descriptions of the activities, each theme in this book provides clear Learning Intentions and extension ideas and activities as Home Links to involve parents/carers in their child's learning.

This title, **Number and Calculating,** particularly supports children's progress towards attaining the Early Learning Goals in the Mathematics and Communication and language areas of learning.

Number concepts are explored through a wide variety of games and play-based activities in everyday contexts, sometimes led by a story or poem. Knowledge and understanding of number is enhanced

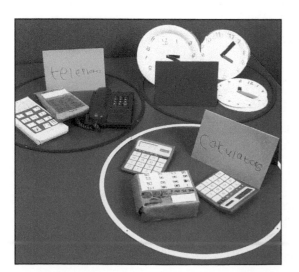

through talking about what is going on. Opportunities are provided for children to practise and improve their skills in counting, mark-making and simple calculations, including sharing. Throughout this book, informal mark-making using a variety of media is explored as part of the emphasis on doing and discussing.

Although this title is organised into themes, many of the activities could stand alone or be interchanged between themes. In order to ensure that the children become comfortable with a range of methods, resources such as number cards, dice and spinners are rarely specific to the activity and can be interchanged as required.

I hope that adults and children alike will enjoy exploring the activities in this book.

Cherri Moseley

Recognising Numbers

Learning Intentions

● To recognise the numerals 1 to 9 in a range of formats.

● To use the number names appropriately.

● To begin to write the numerals 1 to 9.

● To begin to recognise the numbers beyond 9.

● Learn some counting finger rhymes. Accompany the rhymes by showing the appropriate number of fingers each time. Occasionally stop and check the number of fingers, recording the matching numeral on a large whiteboard or paper. Repeat the rhymes with the fingers behind the back, stopping to check that the correct numbers of fingers are shown.

Starting Points

● Put a wooden or solid numeral in a padded envelope or feely bag. Gradually reveal the numeral, asking the children to guess which numeral they think it is. Can the children explain their guesses? Extend the activity by gradually revealing the numeral upside down or sideways.

Exploration

dice

● Join large sheets of paper together. Draw or use tape to make a ladder with ten or more rungs. Make the ladder wide enough for two children to be able to stand on any particular rung at a time. Label each rung with the numerals 1 to 10.

● Show the children how to roll a large spot die and move along the ladder. Take it in turns to roll the die and step along the ladder appropriately. The winner is the first to the top of the ladder. A die with only one, two and three spots will make the game last longer.

- Make a large six by six grid on a piece of A4 paper or card. Using the numerals 1 to 6 only, put a different numeral in each square in random order. Repeat each numeral six times. Provide up to four pots of different-coloured counters and a 1 to 6 die. Play the game by taking it in turns to roll the die and then placing a colour counter on one copy of that numeral. If all the copies of the numeral are covered, then miss a turn. The winner is the first person to get a line of coloured counters stretching from one side to the other (or from top to bottom). Play with just two children at first and ask them to show two more children how to play, and so on.

Free Play

- Put a layer of damp sand in some shallow trays. Attach a different numeral to the end of each tray. Invite the children to practise writing the numeral in the sand.

- Provide a range of jigsaws with a number theme.

Language and Literacy

- Discuss how many children can safely play in each area. Look around the room and support the children to negotiate and reach an agreement.

- Make some signs with the appropriate numeral and that number of children for each area. Draw around a child-shaped cookie cutter to give a clear picture. Decorate the sign to match the area, for example paint the numerals and figures on the sign with glue, then sprinkle with sand while still wet.

Outside

- Set up a parking area for scooters and tricycles. Make a laminated number plate for each vehicle and attach it to the front. Section off a small area of the playground, then mark out smaller parking spaces with chalk and matching number plates. Each vehicle must be parked in the space that matches its number plate.

- Rinse and fill some squeezy bottles with water. Use the water to write numerals on the ground and walls outside, or as a marker for counting outside objects such as flowers and leaves.

Creative

- Make a collage of large numerals for display on the wall using a variety of materials. Cut out the numerals from card and encourage the children to decorate them with vibrant patterns.

- Show the children how to use stencils and templates. Leave some number templates and stencils on a table with a selection of pencils, felt pens and crayons. Encourage the children to use the templates and stencils to help them to draw the numerals and then decorate each numeral. Cut out the numerals and use them as a border for any display with a number theme.

Our World

- Make biscuits in the shape of numerals. Press the correct number of raisins lightly into the surface of each biscuit before baking. Alternatively, bake the biscuits and use a little icing to add the correct number of chocolate drops or small sweets once the biscuits have cooled.

Home Links

Ask parents or carers to:

- examine food and other packaging together to find the number of items in the packet.

What's My Number?

Starting Points

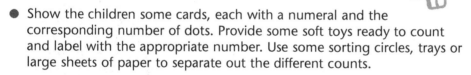

- Show the children some cards, each with a numeral and the corresponding number of dots. Provide some soft toys ready to count and label with the appropriate number. Use some sorting circles, trays or large sheets of paper to separate out the different counts.

- Play the 'Grab Game'. Place a set of small objects (up to ten) inside a decorated 'grab' box with a hole cut in the side or top. A children's shoebox is ideal. Play some music and pass the box around the circle. When the music stops ask the child with the box to feel inside the hole and grab a handful of objects to take out and show the class. Count the objects together and then invite the child who 'grabbed' the objects to pick the correct numeral card.

Exploration

- Prepare a 1 to 6 number track for each child and provide a bowl of counters. Take turns to roll a spot die. Count the number of spots on the die, place that number of counters on the appropriate number on the number track. The winner is the first person to match every number on their track. As the game progresses, ask the children which numbers they still need and how many spaces they have left.

- Make an interactive counting line. Staple some counting bags to the wall or hang on hooks (takeaway-food mini-carrier bags are ideal). Attach a large numeral to the front of each bag. Invite a child to put the correct number of objects in any of the bags, counting out loud as they do so. Ask another child to remove the items, checking that the correct number of items were in the bag. If the bags are not fixed, encourage the children to order them too.

see thn bags

- Working with a small group of children, make a staircase pattern on a pegboard. Start with a single peg in the top left corner of the pegboard. On the next row, add one more peg. Continue until there are ten pegs in the row. On each row count the pegs and emphasise that there is one more peg than in the previous row, for example: 'Five and one more makes six pegs. Let's count them together – one, two, three, four, five, six.' Invite the children to explain the pattern produced.

Free Play

- Prepare some cards with the outline of a different number of buttons drawn on each one. Vary the sizes of the buttons, depending on the collection of buttons available. Label each card with the words 'How many?' Leave a selection of buttons on the table for the children to match to the cards.

Language and Literacy

● Choose a numeral and make a book about that number. Draw a large numeral on the front cover. Inside, draw or stick examples of that number of items. Add the children's writing (or scribe for them).

● Make up a story orally with the children, using objects and numeral cards as props, for example: 'Mr Bear went to the shops to buy three apples. He chose three big, red apples and counted them into the bag, one, two, three.'

Outside

● Set out a line of cones with a spot card attached to each one. Balance a light plastic toy on the top of each cone. Rinse and fill some squeezy bottles with water. Use the water to knock the toys off the cones, as in fairground shooting games. Give instructions such as 'Knock the object off number five.' How many toys can each child knock off with one bottle of water?

● Cut out some cardboard apples or use plastic ones. Attach loops to the apples and hang to the lower branches of trees around the setting. Prepare some numeral cards. Ask a child to pick a card, then run and collect that number of apples from the tree. Use both red and green apples, and once a few children have had a turn ask questions such as: 'How many red apples are on our tree today?'; 'How many green ones?' Extend the questioning to include such questions as: 'How many would be left if one fell off?'

Creative

- Provide a set of construction equipment or linking cubes on a table or mat. Ask the children to make a model from a specific number of pieces, for example ten. Any pieces can be chosen, but the model must contain the correct number of pieces. Make a label for each model, showing who made it and what it is. Display the models with a sign saying 'Look what we can make with 10 cubes!'

- Explore a range of musical instruments. Set up a class orchestra with groups of children playing a particular instrument. Point to each group and show them a numeral card to tell them how many times to shake, blow or strike their instrument. Choose a confident child to take over as conductor.

Our World

- Make a large batch of pizza dough and give each child a chunk to flatten into a pizza shape. Help each child to spread the top with crushed tomato or tomato purée.

- Provide some separate bowls of toppings prepared with pictorial number cards that specify the amount of each topping that can be used, such as two slices of mushroom, three slices of cheese, four olives. The toppings need to be items that can be counted rather than a mass such as grated cheese.

- Encourage the children to read the numeral card and count out the required amount of topping. Arrange the toppings on the pizza and bake. The children could take the pizza home to share.

Home Links

Ask parents or carers to:

- look out for numerals around the home

- ask their child 'How many?' questions frequently.

Language and Literacy

- Set up a writing table with a variety of papers, cards and envelopes. Make a postbox from a box with a slot, covered or painted by the children.

- Encourage the children to write to the occupants of Number Avenue. They must label their envelope with the house number and post it in the postbox.

- At the end of the day, empty each house's letterbox and count the envelopes. Which house has the most letters? Which one has the fewest? Did any house get none?

- Set up a doll's house and provide play people. Count the play people in each room. Are there any rooms with no people in? What number means none? Label each room with a numeral to show how many play people are in that room.

- Move the play people around, and question the children as to how many people are now left in each room.

Outside

- Take the children for a walk around the local area. Look at the different styles of home. Count the windows, doors, chimneys, and so on. Look at the numbering on the doors. Take some photographs, then make a street counting book, illustrated with the photographs taken on the walk.

- Mark out a roadway on the playground. Ensure that all play vehicles such as tricycles and scooters keep to the roadway. Make some large boxes into houses by painting or sticking on windows and doors and adding letterboxes. Add a garage or parking bay. Group the houses along the side of the roadway to make streets, numbering the houses appropriately. Make and deliver parcels to the correct house. Attach numeral cards to scooters and tricycles and encourage the children to park at the house with the same number.

14

Creative

- Create a model village. Cover a large, low table with paper. Help the children to make a suitable road layout, including junctions. Make the houses by turning boxes inside out. Tape each box closed, using masking tape as this can be painted over. Paint the boxes, including windows and doors. Add cars and people and encourage the children to play freely. Include numerals wherever appropriate.

- Use musical instruments to make patterns such as drum–triangle, drum–triangle. Invite one child to play a pattern and another to copy it.

Our World

- Set up a small track with numbered pit stops. Challenge the children to drive remote control cars around the track. Give instructions such as 'Go to pit stop 2.'

- Play a tape of street sounds and ask the children to identify the sounds. Tapes are available commercially or take a tape recorder and microphone on your walk around the local area.

Home Links

Ask parents and carers to:

- take time to listen outside, helping their child to identify the sounds they hear

- help their child to learn his or her address and telephone number.

Numbers All Around

Learning Intentions

- To recognise numbers in the environment.

- To begin to identify the uses of numbers in the environment.

- To become increasingly aware of the range of uses of numbers.

Starting Points

- Ask the children where they have seen numbers. Look around the classroom. What numbers can they see and what are they for? Where else have they seen numbers? Make a number collection. Only items with numbers on can be part of the collection.

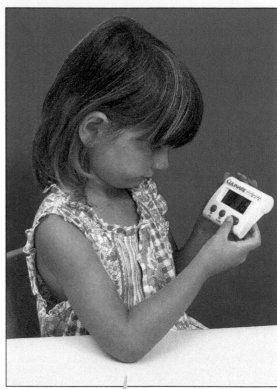

- Show the children a digital timer. Set the timer so that the children can see the numbers continually changing. Watch how the numbers change and count along with the final digit only.

- Set the timer to count down during significant times in the day (such as tidy-up time) and encourage the children to look at it as they complete the activity. Ask the children to stop and stand still immediately the timer has finished.

Exploration

- Make sure that each child in the group can see a calculator. Show the children how to make each number appear. Experiment with different patterns of numbers. Look carefully at how the numbers are made of light bars. Provide paper and pens and calculators for the children to explore freely.

- Draw outlines of telephones and calculators, clearly showing the keypads. On a large example number the keypads correctly. Provide a blank outline and ask the children as a group to fill in the missing numbers. Repeat the exercise with a blank calculator. Leave the calculator and telephone outlines in the Maths area for free play to encourage practice of numeral writing.

- Write each digit of the school telephone number on a blank playing card. Write the number at the top of a large sheet of paper. Working with a small group of children, invite the children to mix up the numbers to create a new telephone number. Collect all the different numbers on the large piece of paper, checking that the new number is not a duplicate.

Free Play

- Set up a number shop. Only items with numbers on can be sold in the shop. Ask the children for suggestions about what the shop might sell – telephones, calculators, remote controls, clocks, menus with prices, shoes and shoeboxes. Give each item a price label and encourage the children to shop or to be the shopkeeper.

- Make a selection of items to add to the number shop. Turn boxes inside out and secure the flaps. Paint or draw on the boxes, as necessary. Cut a door into a large box and add a keypad to turn it into a microwave. Cut a flap in a flatter box and add a number display to turn it into a video recorder. Smaller boxes make good mobile phones or calculators. Use number stickers to make the keypads more realistic.

- Draw a three by three grid on a magnetic board. Provide an example telephone keypad. Write 5 in the centre square on the board. Invite the children to complete the keypad with magnetic numbers.

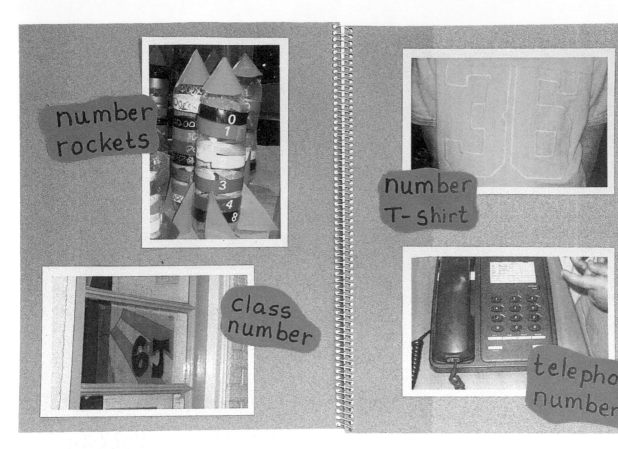

number rockets

number T-shirt

class number

telephone numbers

Language and Literacy

● Collect shoes in a range of sizes. Clearly label the shoes with the appropriate numeral size and place them in order. Discuss the different sizes and who would wear them.

● Use story characters such as Tinkerbell or Thumbelina to help the children to visualise the owner of the smallest shoes. Introduce adult shoe sizes. Compare the sizes of the largest and smallest shoes. What size would a giant need? Again, involve story characters to help the children with their predictions.

● Share fun rhymes such as the nonsense rhyme 'How Many Shoes?' in *Nonsense Counting Rhymes* by Kaye Umansky (published by Oxford University Press).

● Go for a number walk around the school looking for objects with numerals. Take photographs of the objects. Make the photographs into a loose-leafed catalogue or book, organised by the room or area. Add the folder to the number shop and provide order forms to enable the children to order items.

Outside

● Chalk or paint a hopscotch grid outside and teach the children how to play. Show the children how to set a timer for five minutes in order to give more children the opportunity to play the game.

● Play the game 'What's the time, Mr Wolf?'

Creative

- Cut out large numerals matching the ages of the children in the class. Using ink or finger paints in a range of colours, ask each child to choose their favourite colour and decorate the numeral matching their age. Once dry, label each child's prints with their name and add an appropriate title such as 'We are 5!'

- Make calculator numerals with art straws on black paper. Cut each straw into three equal lengths to make them more manageable.

Our World

- Talk to the children about how old they are and what that means. Ask parents to send in a photograph of their child at each age reached to date, starting from zero. Help the children to make a personal timeline, showing their development.

- Sort the objects from the number collection (see Starting Points) into groups. Suggest grouping the items into things that tell the time or timers, switches, and so on. Encourage the children to make their own suggestions.

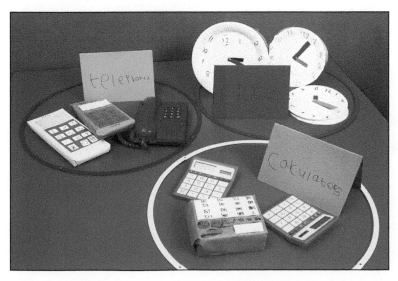

Home Links

Ask parents or carers to:

- point out o'clock times on a clock, particularly at the beginning or end of an activity

- collect items with numbers on to add to the number shop

- help their child to look for numbers at home: 'Which room has the most numbers in it?'; 'Which one has the fewest?'

Ten White Snowmen

Learning Intentions

● To develop understanding of number through rhymes and songs.

Starting Points

● Read the rhyme 'Ten White Snowmen' by John Foster.

● Invent actions, or draw the ten snowmen on the white board, rubbing each out at the appropriate place in the rhyme.

● Act out the rhyme. Provide hats and scarves as props. Encourage the children to leave the line of snowmen in the manner suggested by the rhyme. Use a number line to support the counting, pointing to each number when it occurs in the rhyme.

Exploration

● Draw the outline of ten snowmen on a strip of white paper. Make sufficient copies for the age group. Ask the children to decorate the snowmen so that each one is different. Help the children to number the snowmen from 1 to 10. Use the snowmen strips as the group practises the rhyme.

● Encourage each child to hold the strip with both hands, the left hand holding the 1 end and the right hand holding the 10 end. As the number of snowmen decreases, show the children how to slide their right hand along so that the thumb is always pointing at the correct number of snowmen. When number 1 vanishes, they could simply drop the paper, or fold it over so that no snowmen are visible.

● Make ten snowmen from salt dough. Label the snowmen with the numbers 1 to 10. Put the snowmen on the table randomly. Ask the children to put them in order and recite the numbers from 10 to 1. Muddle up the snowmen and remove one. Ask the children to put them in order and say which one is missing. Count the snowmen, replacing the missing snowman with a clap.

Ten White Snowmen

Ten white snowmen
standing in a line,
One toppled over,
then there were nine.

Nine white snowmen
standing up straight,
One lost his balance,
then there were eight.

Eight white snowmen
in a snowy heaven,
The wind blew one over,
then there were seven.

Seven white snowmen with
pipes made of sticks,
One slumped to the ground,
then there were six.

Six white snowmen
standing by the drive,
One got knocked down,
then there were five.

Five white snowmen
outside the front door,
An icicle fell on one, then
there were four.

Four white snowmen
standing by the tree,
One slipped and fell apart,
then there were three.

Three white snowmen
underneath the yew,
One crumbled overnight,
then there were two.

Two white snowmen
standing in the sun,
One melted right down,
then there was one.

One white snowman
standing all alone,
Vanished without a trace,
then there were none.

John Foster

Free Play

- Break up polystyrene tiles and add the pieces to the water tray to form pretend ice. Provide play people, Arctic and Antarctic creatures.

- Use flour or salt for snow. Spread the pretend snow on an edged tabletop. Provide some play people and vehicles. Cut some lolly sticks in half and glue them with PVA glue to the bottom of play people for skis. Number the play people and have a skiing race. Soak the play people in warm water to remove the skis once the activity is finished.

Language and Literacy

- Record a tape of the children saying the number rhyme. Practise first and encourage the children to speak clearly. Add other favourite rhymes and songs. Leave the tape in the listening corner for the children to enjoy.

Outside

- If it is winter and the weather obliges, a snowfall would be ideal for this rhyme. Make real snowmen, as large as the snow allows. Build snow caves for play people.

- Alternatively, take the opportunity to defrost the fridge or freezer and use the ice, or freeze some water in an assortment of small containers. Collect the chunks of ice in a bowl and take them outside. Hold an ice race. Arrange the children in equal lines of four or more, as appropriate. Place a container with pieces of ice at one end of each line and another empty container at the other end. The pieces of ice must be passed along the line to the new container. As the ice melts, it will become very slippery and will be dropped several times. Either play on grass or allow the children to pick up the largest piece if the dropped piece breaks. The winning team is the one with the most ice left, if any!

Creative

- Make a snowman mobile.
Glue two pompoms or polystyrene balls together. Choose a large one for the body and a smaller one for the head. Use a small strip of material or paper to make a scarf and glue in place. Draw or glue on wobbly eyes, a nose, mouth and some buttons to complete. Tie a length of white cotton to the head. Tie the other end to a wire coat hanger to make a mobile.

- Use empty crisp tubes to make snowmen. Spread the tube with glue and cover it with tufts of cotton wool. Add a strip of fabric for a scarf, about one third of the way down the tube. Add a mouth, eyes and a nose and some buttons or a hat to finish.

- Make real finger puppet snowmen. Lay both hands on the table, palms down. Using face paints, cover the fingers with white paint. Use a washable felt pen to add eyes, a nose, a mouth and some buttons. The children can then enjoy watching the snowmen help with their activities, including acting out the number rhyme.

⚠ **Note:** Check for allergies when using face paints.

- Make up a snowmen dance together.
Loosely tie streamers of white crêpe paper to each child's wrists. Encourage them to raise and lower their arms as they float through the air. Use the music from Raymond Briggs' *The Snowman* (published by Hamish Hamilton Children's Books) to accompany the dance. Watch the video together for ideas.

Our World

- Make ice lollies for all the children from fruit juice. Dilute the juice with an equal quantity of water to ensure that the lollies freeze properly. If you do not have moulds, use small fromage frais containers or ice cube trays. Add a lolly stick once the liquid is partly frozen. Take the lollies out of the freezer a few minutes before use to ensure that the ice does not burn.

Home Links

Ask parents or carers to:

- take home a copy of the number rhyme 'Ten White Snowmen' to learn together.

Number Race

Learning Intentions

- To order a given set of numbers.

- To identify a missing number from a set of numbers.

- To develop understanding of ordinal number.

- To use ordinal numbers in a variety of contexts.

Starting Points

- Put out ten or twenty objects, and model counting them by touching and/or moving each object. Make some deliberate mistakes. Can the children spot the mistakes? Using a puppet to make the mistakes makes this activity more fun!

- Give a different number tile to each child. Ask the children to line up in order.

- Once the children are familiar with ordering, keep a number for yourself or give one to another adult in the room. Can the children tell the adult where they need to be in the line?

- The children sit in a semi-circle in number order. Call out the numbers in counting order. Each child places their tile down when called, then raises it again so that the order can be seen. When collecting the tiles to put them away, talk about having number 1 first, number 2 second, and so on.

- Look at a calendar with the children. Emphasise the link between how the numbers are written on the calendar and how we read them. Discuss with the children when we use words like first, second and third. Talk about the date each day and invite a child to cross it off on the calendar.

Exploration

- Cut out some large numerals. Add arms, legs and faces to make them come alive. Laminate or paint with PVA glue to make them sturdy.

- Create a large, simple scene for the numerals to race through, such as a background of hills, trees and flowers with a winding track. Include a start and finish.

- Display the scene on a wall or board where everyone can reach. Attach Velcro to the back of the numerals and along the track at different intervals.

- Put all the numerals at the start and invite the children to put the numerals in order along the track.

Free Play

- Make some stars with the numbers 1 to 10 on them. Attach some Velcro to the back of each one. Arrange matching pieces of Velcro on a night sky background. Invite the children to put the stars in the sky in the correct order. This is a useful assessment exercise.

- Find wrapping paper with illustrated numbers. Cut out the sections and stick to card. Invite the children to order them by placing them into a set of transparent pockets. Make the pockets from a strip of card and a narrower strip of clear plastic. Glue or staple the plastic to the bottom half of the card. Make sure that it is deep enough to form a pocket and loose enough to slide the cards in and out easily.

Language and Literacy

- Provide a Noah's Ark with a single entrance. Put some of the animals in a queue, ready to enter the ark. Invite the children to line up the animals how they wish. Ask a range of questions, such as: 'Which animal is first in the queue?'; 'Which animal is behind the tiger?'; 'Which animal is in front of the elephant?'

- Set up an arrival ladder near the door. Draw a ladder on a long piece of card or paper. Add rolled paper or cardboard tubing to give a three-dimensional effect. Fix to the wall near the door. Label each rung with the symbol and word for the position. Laminate a name card for each child. When a child arrives, they can fix their name to the next rung on the ladder. During the day, look at the ladder and discuss who arrived first, second and third.

- Use ordinal language to describe the children's positions whenever the opportunity arises, for example when the children line up.

Outside

- Set groups of children some fun challenges that are appropriate to their age and the items available. Ask questions such as: 'Who will be the first person to bring me a blade of grass?'; 'Who will be the first person to ride a bike to the playhouse?' Tell the children who was first, second or third.

- Place hoops on the ground and ask the children to take it in turns to throw a large ball into the hoop. Allow each child three attempts and give a running commentary on their first, second and third throws, using ordinal language.

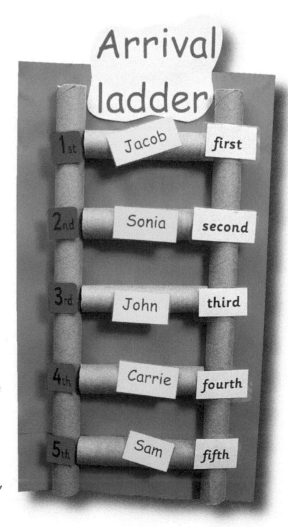

Creative

- Make medals for the children. Cut out a large circle for each child from coloured card. Write the child's name in the middle of the circle. Punch some holes around and near the edge. Use plastic needles and wool or thin ribbon to sew around the circle. Punch a hole near the top of the medal and thread sufficient elastic or ribbon through the hole to allow the medal to be worn as a necklace. Add 1st, 2nd or 3rd to the medals and use in free play.

- Ask the children to shuffle a pack of numeral cards. Pick a card and then make that numeral in cookie dough. Pick a different card and make a different numeral. After everyone has had a go, bake the dough in the shape of numerals and display in order before eating.

Our World

- Float small plastic toys such as bears, dinosaurs or vehicles in the water tray. Provide large plastic tweezers or tongs and a one-minute sand timer. Challenge each child to pick out as many objects as they can, using the tweezers only, in one minute.

- Talk to the children about getting dressed in the morning. Which item of clothing do they put on first? Is it the same for everyone? Does it matter? Are there some clothes that have to be put on in a certain order?

- Arrange some pipes of equal length side by side, supported at one end to tilt the pipe and allow objects to roll down freely. Encourage the children to have pipe races by rolling items down the pipes. Which items appear first, second and third?

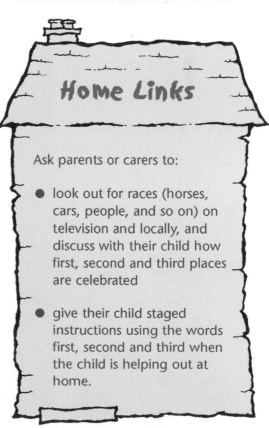

Home Links

Ask parents or carers to:

- look out for races (horses, cars, people, and so on) on television and locally, and discuss with their child how first, second and third places are celebrated

- give their child staged instructions using the words first, second and third when the child is helping out at home.

Ten Black Dots

Learning Intentions

- To count a range of items accurately in a variety of contexts.

- To develop touching or moving objects during counting to improve accuracy.

- To use stories to develop understanding of counting.

- To encourage instant recognition of standard die and domino spot patterns.

Starting Points

- Partly fill some boxes with different sets of objects. Choose a child to pick a box. Ask them to lift it and gently shake it to help them to guess (estimate) how many things are inside. Encourage the child to open the box and count. Look for different methods of counting, such as tipping out the contents and counting back into the box or counting by moving the items out of the box one at a time.

- Collect a pile of large objects (soft toys, bricks, and so on) on the carpet where all the children can see them. Ask the children to estimate how many objects there are in the pile. Give them a card showing the amount they guessed in dots with the matching numeral.

- Choose a child to count the objects by removing one item from the pile and moving it to a second pile. Ask the children to help by counting aloud. Did anyone guess correctly?

- Read the story *Ten Black Dots* by Donald Crews (published by Mulberry Books). Count the black dots on each page. Look at how the dots are used in each picture. Discuss how the children could use black dots in their own pictures.

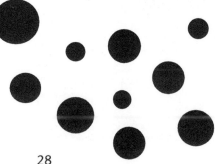

2 and 4 makes 6

4 and 2 makes 6

3 and 3 makes 6

6 and 0 makes 6

2 and 4 makes 6

5 and 1 makes 6

Ladybird sixes

Exploration

- Paint some large ladybirds with a black line down their backs to show their wing cases. Cut out some black spots. Decide on a number, for example six. Each ladybird must have that number of spots. Show the children how to arrange the spots on the two halves of the ladybird's back. Ask the children to find lots of different ways to put six spots on each ladybird. When the children have finished, display each ladybird with its matching addition sum, surrounded by large leaves.

- Play spot snap. Make sets of spot cards one to six in standard die and domino patterns using blank playing cards. Combine two or three sets to play snap with small groups of children. Although the children may need to count the number of dots initially, encourage instant recognition of the number of spots as they become more familiar with the cards.

- Ask the children to match the cards from the previous activity to numerals on a large 1 to 6 number track. Have a race against a one-minute sand timer. Who can match all the cards before the sand runs out? Who is the fastest?

- Make a set of different-coloured one to six dot cards. Bury the appropriate number of coloured counters in the sand tray and ask the children to find and match the coloured counters to the matching colour cards.

29

Free Play

● Laminate pictures of creatures that usually have spots, but with the spots missing – for example, ladybirds, dogs, leopards and snakes. Provide pens so that the children can draw on their own spot patterns. Encourage the children to count the number of spots on their animal.

● Make some simple dot-to-dot pictures from line drawings. Add equally spaced dots to fill the gaps. Introduce zero as the starting point. Number the dots as appropriate to the group of children. Leave a selection of dot-to-dots on a table with some pencils and a number line for support if necessary.

Language and Literacy

● Discuss counting with the children. Talk about how they count, focusing on moving the item as it is counted. Ask how they could count items that cannot be moved, such as claps, finger clicks, jumps and nods. Challenge each child to carry out a particular action a given number of times. Generate the number by rolling a large spot die or by turning over a spot card.

● When the children are more confident, ask them to try counting in their heads whilst another child jumps or claps, giving a 'thumbs up' at the end if they think they know the correct number.

● Introduce zero and explain its meaning. Use a number line to show its position before the number 1. Learn number rhymes that count backwards to reinforce zero's meaning as none. Practise writing 0 in the air.

Outside

● Chalk or stick large dot patterns on the walls and floor outside in the playground. Give the children fun challenges such as: 'Run to number three'; 'Hop to number four'; 'Stand by number five and clap five times.'

● Show the children how to play a game of marbles. Provide a class set of large marbles so that anyone can play. If the children find the marbles difficult to use, play with small balls instead.

Creative

- Provide large and small black dots for the children to incorporate into pictures. When each picture is complete, ask the children to count how many black dots they have used. Help each child to write a sentence to accompany their picture – 'I used 3 black dots in my picture'. Display the pictures and sentences together. Ask questions about the pictures, such as: 'Who used the most dots?'; 'Who used the fewest dots?'; 'Who used more dots than Jo?' Add the questions to the display.

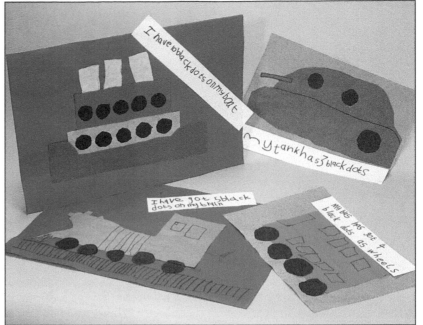

- Make dot mobiles from unwanted or free CDs. Turn the CD over and decorate the clear side. Use coloured, self-adhesive spots or glue on small pieces of fabric, brightly coloured paper or other recycled materials. Tie wool or string through the central hole to make a tail, as on a kite. Make sure some of the original CD is still visible. Hang the discs back to back near a window to reflect the light. When the window is open, the CDs will be light enough to respond to any breeze.

Our World

- Examine each other's coats. Count buttons to find out who has the most/fewest. Look at the sewing holes in the buttons. How many holes are there in each button? Who has the most/fewest number of holes?

- Examine different buttons under a microscope. Show the children how apparently smooth buttons have a rough texture under the microscope. Look at the holes too. Examine other everyday objects under the microscope. Encourage the children to look at the textures and compare what they see under the microscope with what they see normally.

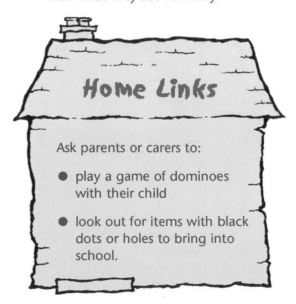

Home Links

Ask parents or carers to:

- play a game of dominoes with their child

- look out for items with black dots or holes to bring into school.

How Many Snails?

Starting Points

- Make a simple outdoor scene on a large board within easy reach of the children. Create snails and butterflies to add to the scene. Make the snails by coiling string onto paper liberally painted with glue. Once dry, paint each snail using just one or two colours. Make the butterflies by painting one half of a butterfly shape and folding the paper over to create the other half.

- Once dry, add some butterflies and snails to the scene using mouldable soft putty. Ask questions such as: 'How many blue butterflies are there?'; 'How many green snails can you see?' Invite children to come to the front to count particular items. Encourage touching each item as it is counted. Change the creatures in the scene and repeat.

Learning Intentions

- To count a range of items accurately in a variety of situations.

- To develop touching or moving objects during counting to improve accuracy.

- To recognise that the order of the items being counted does not matter.

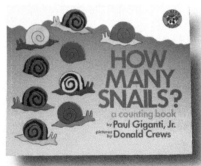

HOW MANY SNAILS?
a counting book
by Paul Giganti, Jr.
pictures by Donald Crews

- Read the story *How Many Snails?*, a counting book by Paul Giganti, Jr (published by HarperCollins). Model touching each object as you count it to help the children to answer the questions in the book. Ask for volunteers to answer a question, ensuring that each object is touched as it is counted.

Exploration

- Roll modelling material such as plasticine or clay into long sausage shapes and then coil them to make snails. Make the snails in a range of colours or paint them. Display on a tabletop with foliage and rocks. Add questions to the display, such as: 'How many snails are on the rocks?'; 'How many red snails can you see?', and so on.

- How much is a handful? Use cubes or other items that are not too small in order to prevent the count from becoming large. Invite predictions before taking a handful. Count the objects that have been picked up. To record, the children could draw around their hand on a named paper plate. Next to the hand, draw one of the selected items and label it with the number in the handful.

- Useful extension activities include asking each child to compare their own right and left hands. Which one can hold the most/fewest objects? Offer a range of different-sized items to pick up. Can the children modify their predictions appropriately? Challenge the children to pick up a specific number: 'Can you pick up exactly four conkers?'

- Prepare some picture attribute cards for threading beads, buttons or other small equipment with differences in shape and colour. Take it in turns to roll a spot die and pick up an attribute card. Collect the appropriate number and type of beads, threading them onto their lace or piece of string.

Free Play

- Set up a counting table with bowls of items to be counted and empty bowls to count into. Craft shops often sell small items such as ladybirds, butterflies and bees that can be used as fun counting items. Ask the children questions when visiting the area, such as: 'How many green ones are there?'; 'How many round ones?'; 'How many with stripes?'

33

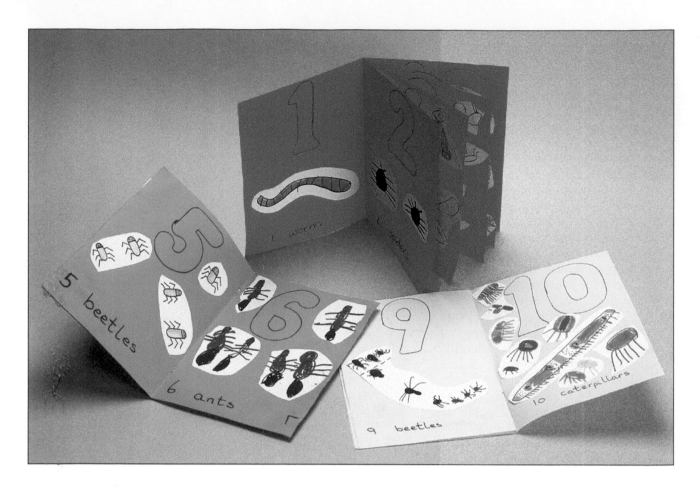

Language and Literacy

● Use the outdoor scene (see Starting Points), and encourage the children to ask more complicated questions, such as 'How many butterflies are there with red and blue wings?'

● Make minibeast counting books. Fold three sheets of A4 paper in half and staple or sew the centre to make a book. Start with a large number 1 on the inside front cover and continue to number 10 on the inside back cover. On each page, draw the appropriate number of one kind of minibeast. At the bottom of each page, either the child or an adult can scribe a caption.

Outside

● Either place a large, shallow container near a wall or tape a hoop or piece of strong paper to the ground to form a pond. Invite the children to throw green beanbags (frogs) into the pond. Count the beanbags in the pond to find the score. Use shaped beanbags if available. Add some paper or card lily pads to the pool. Award a point for each frog on a lily pad.

● Arrange six lily pads, each with a beanbag resting on it, with enough space to roll a ball between. Two children take it in turns to try to roll a ball to each other without disturbing the frogs. Award one point for each successful roll.

Creative

- On a large sheet of paper, paint large and small spirals in a range of colours. Count the spirals. How many large/small/green/blue ones are there?

- Make cone spirals from card circles. Make a single cut to the centre of the card circle and overlap about a quarter of the circle to form a cone. Glue or tape the edges in place. Wrap thick wool, twine or string around the cone to give a spiral effect. Alternatively, coil the wool onto paper plates that have been liberally painted with glue.

Our World

- Collect some garden snails and green foliage. Place on a covered tabletop or shallow tray for the children to observe. Have a selection of magnifying glasses available and encourage the children to look closely at the snails and study how they move, eat, and so on. Make sure that the children wash their hands after touching the snails. Always return the snails to the wild after each session.

- Borrow some large African snails for the children to observe and care for as class pets. If the snails are in the classroom for more than a day or two, make some simple, regular observations of their movements and eating habits. Use these observations to try to work out what the snails like to eat and when they are most active.

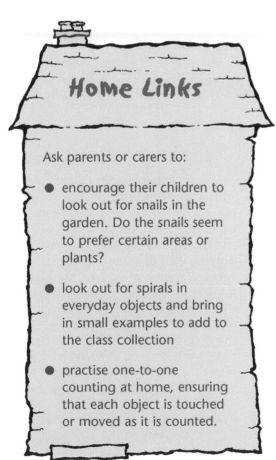

Home Links

Ask parents or carers to:

- encourage their children to look out for snails in the garden. Do the snails seem to prefer certain areas or plants?

- look out for spirals in everyday objects and bring in small examples to add to the class collection

- practise one-to-one counting at home, ensuring that each object is touched or moved as it is counted.

- Collect objects with spirals and discuss how they might be grouped. Some suggestions include:
  - natural objects such as seashells, ammonite fossils and snail shells
  - man-made equipment such as drill bits, screws, ropes and cables
  - plants such as ferns, pine cones, seed heads and Romanesco broccoli
  - household objects such as woven tablemats and decorative plates.

Adders

Learning Intentions

- To be able to say the number that is one more or two more than a given number.

- To begin to relate addition to combining two and later three groups of objects.

- To begin to relate addition to counting on.

- To be able to find the total number of objects in two groups through a variety of methods.

Starting Points

- Talk to the children about how old they are. Ask them how that number changes when they have a birthday. Use the words 'one more'. Ask some of the children how old they will be when they have had one more birthday. Use a number line to show the children 'one more' for each of their ages.

- Use a cotton reel string to explore 'one more'. Thread ten cotton reels onto a string. Count to a chosen number, generated by a card, moving the reels along the string in unison with the counting. When the chosen number has been reached, ask the children how many there will be if one more reel moves along the string to join the others. Repeat for different numbers, inviting children to hold the string and move the reels as everyone counts together. Ten large, preferably identical beads could be used instead of reels.

Exploration

- Play a selection of board games such as snakes and ladders to develop counting-on skills.

- Set up a hoop or sorting circle with a set of six well-spaced objects inside. Lay a stick in various positions across the circle to partition the six objects into two groups, such as three and three, two and four, and so on. Take care not to touch any of the objects so that the children can see that nothing has changed. Ask how many objects there are in total each time. Invite various children to move the stick to a new position to create another six sum and say the matching number sentence, for example: 'three and three makes six', or 'two and four is six altogether'.

Make pairs of flat counting bases for creature counters, for example holes for mice, leaves for ladybirds, lily pads for frogs or flower heads for bees and butterflies. Turn a spinner and place that amount of creatures on one base. Spin again and place the amount shown on the other base. Show the children how to find out how many there are altogether. Demonstrate moving all the creatures onto one base, counting them as they are moved, in order to find the total.

Give each child a spot die and a numeral die. After rolling both dice, encourage each child to count on from the numeral. Model putting the numeral in your head and counting on by pointing to each dot, then say the addition sum. Provide counters and a number line for support if necessary.

Free Play

Make laminated creatures with detachable legs or tentacles. Punch a hole in the top of each leg and holes on the two opposite sides of the creature's body. Use treasury tags to attach the legs or tentacles to the body. Encourage the children to attach the legs or tentacles as they wish. Ask them how many legs or tentacles there are on each side of the body and how many altogether, linking the answers into an addition sum. Make a series of creatures with detachable legs or tentacles to explore addition to eight, six and four.

Arrange a table with sets of interlocking items such as links and bricks. Invite the children to 'add 1 more' each time they pass the table. Near the end of the session look at how tall the tower is or how long the chain has become.

Language and Literacy

- Share a variety of stories that involve addition, for example *The Greedy Triangle* by Marilyn Burns (published by Scholastic). This story is about an unhappy triangle who feels life would be far more interesting if he could only have one more side. *The Shape of Things* by Dayle Ann Dodds (published by Walker Books) is a story about how shapes become much more when you add to them.

- Use plastic shapes to explore the pictures created when reading the books with the children.

Outside

- On a soft surface such as grass, make a 'snake pit' with obstacles (like tunnels) for the children to explore as human snakes. The children must slither over, under and through the equipment without standing, kneeling or crawling.

- Ask the children to draw large snakes in the playground, on the walls as well as the floor. Add numerals in patterns on their backs. Invite the children to make up their own games using the number snakes.

- Take a parachute outside and ask the children to hold the edges tightly. Show the children how to lift and lower their arms to raise and lower the parachute. Practise making waves. When the children can work together to control the parachute, add a ball. Work together to make the ball travel around the circle. Tell the children they can have one more ball if they say how many balls there would be altogether. Repeat with another ball. A large, round tablecloth or piece of fabric could be used instead of a parachute, but they are not quite so flexible. The fabric from a broken golf umbrella could be used for small groups.

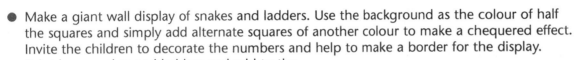

Creative

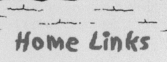

- Make a giant wall display of snakes and ladders. Use the background as the colour of half the squares and simply add alternate squares of another colour to make a chequered effect. Invite the children to decorate the numbers and help to make a border for the display. Paint large snakes and ladders and add to the chequered board.

- Paint a line sum. Using two different colours, paint two groups of lines. When the children have finished, count the different-coloured lines and check the total together. Some children might be able to paint the addition sum on their paper.

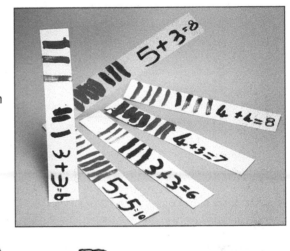

Our World

- Some people keep snakes as pets. Invite an owner to bring in a snake for the children to examine. Invite those who feel able to stroke the snake to do so gently and ask them to try to describe the feel of its skin.

Home Links

Ask parents or carers to:

- look out for opportunities to add up groups of objects at home, for example different foods at mealtimes

- ask 'How many would there be if there was one more?' when handling a small number of objects together.

39

Ten Seeds

- Start with empty creature-counting sticks. Use number cards or a die to show the children how many creatures to put on their stick. Invite the children to put the appropriate number of creatures on their counting stick. Check everyone has the correct amount. Take the creatures off one at a time, checking how many are left each time. If the creatures are different colours, extend the activity by taking off all of one particular colour and asking how many are left.

Starting Points

- Make creature-counting sticks from a length of square dowel. Glue Velcro at suitable intervals along the stick and attach creature counters such as bees, ladybirds or butterflies. Count the creatures on a particular stick together. Take one away and ask the children how many are left. Use language such as 'one fewer' and remind the children of the order of the counting numbers.

- Read the story *Ten Seeds* by Ruth Brown (published by Andersen Press). Discuss what is happening to the seeds in each picture, drawing out language such as 'take away' and 'one fewer'.

Exploration

- Lay out ten cubes in a row. Make a 1 to 10 number track the same length as the row of cubes. Match up the row of cubes and the track, making sure that the cubes do not obscure the numbers. Count the cubes and take one away. Ask the children how many are left. Count them together to check. Extend the activity by taking two away. As the children's confidence develops, repeat the activity without the support of the number track.

- Provide a 1 to 6 spinner, a 7 to 12 die, and a tray of sunflower seeds. Roll the 7 to 12 die and collect that many seeds from the tray. Spin the spinner and take that many seeds away from the collection. How many seeds are left? Make the activity more interesting by explaining that the children are mice, collecting food for their families or birds eating the seeds. If possible, provide each child with an appropriate puppet to use as they collect and take away the seeds.

- Make some simple paper flowers and attach each one to a bendy straw, with the bend near the top. Use plastic containers as vases, with pebbles in the bottom to stabilise them. Halve a set of 1 to 9 number cards with 1 to 4 in one pack, 5 to 9 in the other. Shuffle each pack. Turn over a card from the high number pack. Each child puts this number of flowers in their vase. Turn over a card from the lower number pack. Each child must bend over that number of flowers at the bendy part, so that the flower appears broken. How many flowers are left?

Free Play

- Set up a seed-sorting centre. Collect packets of seeds, both empty and full. Cut out illustrations from seed catalogues and glue them to envelopes to increase the supply. Label some boxes appropriately, for example fruit, vegetables and flowers, and invite the children to sort the seed packets.

- Invite some children to sort the vegetable seeds further, for example by vegetable colour. Provide boxes, card and pens for the children to decide their own sorting criteria and make their own labels.

Language and Literacy

- Revisit the book *Ten Seeds* by Ruth Brown. One seed or seedling is lost on each page due to the actions of a particular creature. Make up similar subtraction stories. With an adult acting as scribe, record the stories in a book illustrated by the children.

- Share the book *One Child One Seed* by Kathryn Cave (published by Frances Lincoln). Show the children a pumpkin like the one in the book. Cut it open and compare it with the photographs in the book. Count some of the seeds. If pumpkins are not available, butternut squash could be used.

Six shoots,

There are six shoots and mole comes along and takes one for a sun hat.

one mole.

- Follow a recipe to make pumpkin pie. Invite the children to try the pie and share their comments.

Outside

- Clear a small area of stones and plants or shrubs. Use the stones or some pebbles to mark out a simple design. Sow suitable seeds or plant bedding plants next to the pebbles to reproduce the design. Choose plants that produce flowers in a variety of colours. Use growbags, tubs or old sinks in a sunny spot if there is no available growing area.

- Check the plants regularly and water if necessary. As the flowers begin to open, ask the children to count how many there are of each colour. Keep a record and compare the numbers as they grow, then dwindle, asking if there are more or fewer each day.

- Ask some flower sums, such as: 'How many yellow ones are there?'; 'If two yellow flowers were broken, how many yellow ones would be left?'

Creative

- Cut out some card circles to use as the centre of a flower. Provide a selection of large seeds to glue onto the circles. Spread a liberal layer of glue on each circle and add the desired selection of seeds. Add paper petals and a stick for a stem to complete the flower. When dry, count the seeds. Ask questions such as: 'How many seeds are there?'; 'How many would there be if a mouse came and took one (or two) away?'

Our World

- Examine a sunflower, or other flower head, with seeds large enough to be counted easily. Use a large, detailed picture and an adult-sized handful of seeds if a flower head is not available. Ask the children to estimate how many seeds there are, then count them.

Our sunflower had 127 seeds!

- Count the seeds in tens. Stick each ten, either in a line or group, to a large piece of paper. Show the children how to count in tens to a hundred. If necessary, mount each hundred on a separate piece of paper and label it. Count the number of hundreds, tens and units and show the children how to write the number. Alternatively, cut a large marrow or pumpkin open. Wash and count the seeds as above.

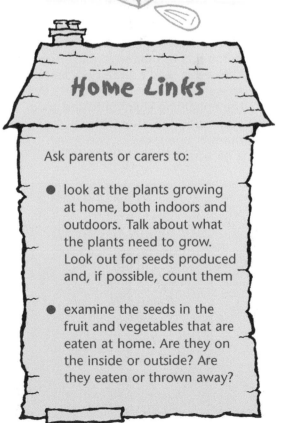

Home Links

Ask parents or carers to:

- look at the plants growing at home, both indoors and outdoors. Talk about what the plants need to grow. Look out for seeds produced and, if possible, count them

- examine the seeds in the fruit and vegetables that are eaten at home. Are they on the inside or outside? Are they eaten or thrown away?

Monster Maths

Learning Intentions

- To be able to say the number that is one fewer or two fewer than a given number.

- To begin to relate subtraction to taking away and counting back.

- To begin to relate subtraction to taking a smaller group of objects away from the initial group.

- Ask ten children to form a live number line, standing in any order. Give each child a large number label to wear, or use number T-shirts. Ask the remaining children to sort them into order. Talk about who is the number one fewer or two fewer than a particular child.

Starting Points

- Hang ten items on a wire coat hanger. Use decorated pegs, key rings or anything that will slide. Tape a piece of card to one end of the hanger so that it can be flipped over to hide part of the hanger. Count the items together. Spread the items along the hanger, so that when the card is flipped over, one item is hidden.

- Count again and pretend to have lost one item. Search for it nearby until a child points out that it is still on the hanger. Reveal the item. Hide different amounts, beginning with just one or two. Ask the children to tell you how many are left. Verbalise the subtraction sum in a variety of ways, for example: 'Ten key rings, two are hiding so that leaves eight.'

Exploration

- Use sheets of sandpaper as bases to explore subtraction. Tear or cut the sheets into rough triangles. Glue two sides of each triangle to a base sheet, with the longest (third) side curved up to form a small cave mouth. Use the caves for hiding small items, for example hide ten small shells. Count how many shells are left. Show the children how to use the information to find out how many shells are hidden, for example ten shells with four shells visible: 'Ten take away four is six, so six shells must be hidden.'

- Collect ready-meal containers with two sections. Make a simple bridge from a strip of card with both long edges folded up. Tape the bridge to the carton to join the two sections. Ask each child to take a specific number of marbles and put them in one section. Ask the children how many marbles would be left if three escaped over the bridge into the other section. Predict and check by helping the marbles to escape over the bridge. Count each section of marbles. Help the children to verbalise the subtraction sum. Repeat for different numbers.

Free Play

- Dress up as monsters! Make monster headbands and use a variety of clothes, including cloaks, to help the children to become monsters.

- Put some pebbles and sea monsters in the bottom of the water tray. If you do not have any suitable monsters, give the children some old plasticine to make their own. Add some boats with fishing nets and invite the children to try to catch a sea monster. Use string bags from washing tablets or small-item laundry bags as nets for the boats. Alternatively, give the children pond-dipping nets.

Language and Literacy

- Make mini hairy monsters. Cut out a basic template and decorate with wool, string, paper or anything that gives a 'hairy' effect. Add wobbly eyes. Mount each monster on a stick. Build a tabletop wall using boxes or construction equipment. Sing 'Ten hairy monsters sitting on the wall ...' to the tune of 'Ten green bottles', using the mini-monsters and wall to add actions to the singing.

- Read *Monster Math* by Grace Maccarone (published by Scholastic). Invite the children to act out the story. Alternatively, make up a short, simple monster adventure story, with one monster leaving the group to do something else until there are none left. Start from 20, 12 or ten, as appropriate to the children. For example:

Ten hairy monsters
*   went to the park,*
One skipped away,
*   now there are nine ...*

Outside

- Hold a monster hunt. Draw a simple monster on a card. Photocopy ten or 12 monsters, numbering each monster then laminating it. Punch a hole and add string for hanging. Before the children come outside, hide the monsters in a variety of places. As the children find the monsters, ask them to order the numbers to find out if there are any missing.

- Blow up 12 balloons (or more, as appropriate to the group of children) and add short, coloured strings or ribbons. Release the balloons outside and invite the children to chase and catch them. Choose a day with some wind, but not enough to blow the balloons away. Inevitably, some balloons will burst. At the end of the outdoor session, count how many balloons are left and work out how many 'escaped'.

- Make shadow monsters. Ask the children to work together to make a shadow monster with six arms or three legs, and so on.

Creative

● Cut out large, simple 'monster' shapes from plain or coloured paper. Shred a few sheets of similar-coloured paper. Paint each monster with PVA glue and cover with matching shredded paper. Once dry, add eyes, mouth, nose and ears, as preferred. Paint bricks on large sheets of paper. Display the hairy monsters on and around the wall with numeral labels.

● Make binoculars to use on the monster hunt. Glue or staple two cardboard tubes together, side by side, and decorate.

Our World

● Use sorting circles or hoops to mark out a patch of grass for the children to examine in pairs. Give the children a magnifying glass and encourage them to lie down next to the circle. Ask them to use the magnifying glass to help them to be explorers, looking for the tiny 'monsters' (insects) that we don't normally notice.

Home Links

Ask parents or carers to:

● collect ready-meal containers with two sections

● visit the zoo or seashore, looking out for unusual creatures.

Picnic Time

Learning Intentions

- To relate addition to combining two or three groups of objects.

- To relate addition to counting on.

- To be able to find the total number of objects in two groups by a variety of methods.

- To relate subtraction to taking away and counting back.

Starting Points

- Set up a tray of mixed, familiar picnic objects. Count the objects together and examine each one to ensure that the children know what each object is. When the children are familiar with the objects and know how many there are, cover the tray with a cloth and use a puppet to burrow under the cloth and take an object away.

- Uncover the tray and count the objects again to find out how many are missing. Can the children identify the missing object? Once the object has been identified, return it to the tray. Repeat with the puppet removing one, two or three objects.

- Ask the children to work out how many objects are missing and to say the subtraction sum, for example: 'We had ten things, seven are left, so three are missing.' Can they recall which items are missing? The puppet could count the objects as it returns them to the tray, saying the addition sum to return to the correct number of objects, for example: 'Seven things on the tray, here's three back, so now there are ten again.'

Exploration

- Lay a tablecloth out on the floor. Give each child a fabric placemat to mark their working area. Use picnic items as the counting objects. Ask one child to select some items and arrange them on their placemat. Count the items together. Explore different arrangements and patterns produced by adding or taking away items from the placemat.

- Continue to explore the number of items by separating a fixed amount into two and then three groups. Add them together in a variety of ways, confirming that the total remains the same.

- Ask each child to collect all their items together again. Hide the items, one at a time, under the placemat. Show the children how to count backwards from the appropriate number until all the items have been hidden and they have counted back to zero.

Free Play

- Set up a sandwich bar. Collect takeaway sandwich boxes and empty drinks cartons. Wash if necessary, reseal and price the items appropriately. Display the items on a table, along with a selection of salt-dough cakes. Provide a till, small bags for the cakes and small takeaway carrier bags. The shopkeeper can pack the chosen items in a takeaway bag and collect the money. Alternatively, use a large basket for a mobile sandwich delivery service.

Language and Literacy

- Talk to the children about inviting their parents and carers to join them at a picnic. Discuss what they would need to know to make sure they came to the correct place at the appropriate time. Plan the place, date and time together. Turn the information into an invitation and give each child a copy to take home. Make a poster to display at arrival and collection time.

- Ask the children what they would like to eat and drink at the picnic. Discuss the need to choose two or three different types of sandwiches and drinks so that everyone can have something they like. Draw up a menu together. Copy the menu and ask some children to illustrate or decorate them.

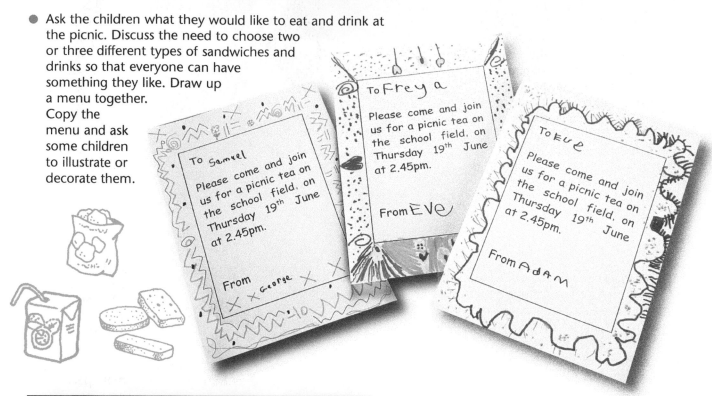

To Samuel
Please come and join us for a picnic tea on the school field, on Thursday 19th June at 2.45pm.

From George

To Freya
Please come and join us for a picnic tea on the school field, on Thursday 19th June at 2.45pm.

From Eve

To Eve
Please come and join us for a picnic tea on the school field, on Thursday 19th June at 2.45pm.

From Adam

Outside

- If there is a snack time, hold it outside as a picnic if possible. Ask the children to help collect everything necessary – drinking cups, fruit, biscuits, and so on. Check that there is enough for everyone by counting the relevant items. When clearing up, count items such as cups again to check that all have been collected.

- Have a picnic basket and blanket ready to use. Children can help prepare the basket for four people, collecting the appropriate number of cups, plates, play food, and so on.

- Make a play tent from canes and a large sheet of fabric. Tie two canes together near one end. Pull the opposite ends apart to make an X shape. Do the same again. Add another cane across the top of the two X shapes to form the basic frame. Lay a large cloth across the top and peg to the four legs. Provide a blanket for inside the tent and any other equipment the children might request. Encourage the children to play in and around the tent.

Creative

- Make model tents. Glue three rows of eight lolly sticks to a piece of paper. Cut the paper close to the sticks on three sides, leaving a few centimetres of paper clear at one end. Make sure the sides of the lolly sticks in each row are touching but not overlapping. Leave a small space between each of the three rows to allow the paper to bend. Once dry, fold the paper to form a triangular prism (tent) shape and glue down the overlapping paper. Decorate the outside of the tent with fabric and cut a piece for the tent floor. Use play people to create a camping scene.

Our World

- Hold a celebration picnic. Invite parents and carers.

- Prepare the food and drink together for the picnic. Cut sandwiches into different shapes. If using squash, experiment with making it stronger or weaker. Sample the results and choose the appropriate strength. Arrange the food and drink on a large table so that people can help themselves.

- Invite the children to decorate the edges of the paper plates for the picnic. Many paper plates have fluted edges that can be coloured in alternate sequence using pens or crayons. Make paper 'cuffs' for plastic or polystyrene cups from strips of paper. Decorate and tape to the cups.

Home Links

Ask parents or carers to:

- collect takeaway sandwich packets for the sandwich bar

- contribute a specific item for the picnic

- Come to the picnic!

Two By Two

Learning Intentions

- To begin to count in steps of two, five and ten.

- To begin to understand the concept of equal grouping.

- To begin to relate doubling to 'two lots'.

Starting Points

- Introduce the idea of two lots of something by looking at how many fingers on two hands, how many toes on two feet, how many noses on two people, and so on. Explain that two lots of something are called double. Play the doubles game. Roll a large die and double the number shown.

- Ask the children to show two fingers. Show them how to count in twos by repeatedly counting the two fingers, touching each finger in turn if necessary. Encourage the children to say the number corresponding to the first finger very quietly, but to say the second finger number normally. The children will quickly progress to counting in twos.

Exploration

- Make a shoebox creature. Score the lid about a third of the way along from the short end and fold to make a mouth. Glue white zigzag paper or card teeth to the short end of the lid and to the box beneath to make a mouth. Add eyes and pointed ears.

- Play 'Feed Henry'. Explain to the children that Henry eats two cubes each day. Say the days of the week, while getting different children to feed Henry two cubes per day. Empty Henry and count the total cubes eaten in a week.

- Take a handful of cubes and help the children to join the cubes in twos and discover how many days of food there would be to feed Henry. Repeat using different amounts of cubes.

- Prepare some cubes by joining them in rows of one, two and three. Make several of each. Use a coloured die labelled with sides 1, 2 or 3 and a spinner with numbers 1 to 5. Roll the die and select a corresponding tower. Turn the spinner to find how many towers to collect. Ask the children to work out how many cubes they have altogether, without breaking up the rows. Encourage the children to count in twos or more, as appropriate.

- Sort creatures by the number of legs they have. Ask the children to put three cows in a line. How many legs are there in that line? Repeat with different numbers and types of animals, including people and birds. If animal stamps are available, record by putting the appropriate number of stamps in a line on a piece of paper with the total number of legs written at the end of the line.

Free Play

- Make patterns on pegboards with repeated groups of two, three or four. Leave enough space at the end for the children to continue the pattern. Encourage the children to make up their own grouped repeating patterns.

- Label some paper plates with the even numbers from 2 to 20 and 0, including some duplicates. Set out the plates on a table with a mixed selection of creatures, including farm and zoo animals, birds and people. Ask the children to put the correct number of legs on each plate.

Language and Literacy

- Look out for number rhymes that help the children to count in groups, both forwards and backwards. Use well-known rhymes such as 'Ten fat sausages' and new ones like 'Six little fish' in *Ten Little Fingers* by Louise Binder Scott (published by LDA). Sing appropriate songs such as 'The animals went in two by two'.

- Read 'Caterpillar Pete' in *Poems to Count On* by Sandra Liatsos (published by Scholastic). Say the rhyme together. Make a giant caterpillar by asking children to line up behind each other while holding onto the waist of the person in front. Count one side together and work out how many shoes, slippers or flippers the caterpillar needs. Make up another version for gloves.

Outside

- Take some hoops outside. Spread the hoops around on the floor. Call out a number, and that number of children must stand inside each hoop. Any hoop with the wrong number of people in it will be taken away and those children will be out of this round of the game.

- Talk about how many children are left after each turn. Call out a variety of numbers until there is only one hoop left. Choose the last number according to the number of children left in the game.

- Count the wheels on the tricycles, bikes or other large, wheeled vehicles. Park some of the tricycles in a line and ask the children how many wheels there are in the line. Invite them to estimate first. Repeat with a vehicle that has a different number of wheels.

Creative

- Cut some strips of paper in a range of colours but all the same width. Tape or staple strips to a piece of backing paper, leaving a little space between each strip to make weaving easier. Show the children how to weave the coloured strips under and over the taped strips. Ask the children to explore the pattern produced when they weave under or over one, two or three strips. Trim the end of the strips and staple in place. Display the weaving with appropriate comments about the grouping of the strips.

- Make individual shoebox creatures. Provide a variety of materials and encourage the children to be creative. Score the lid a third of the way along from the short end and fold to make a mouth or use the long end for a wider mouth. Add eyes and ears. What does it eat? How much does it eat in a day, a week? Display the creatures with their names and eating habits.

My name is Daisy.
I eat 2 shells every day.
How many shells do I eat in a week?

My name is Fergus.
I eat 3 pegs every day.
How many pegs do I eat in 4 days?

My name is Rolly.
I eat 3 beads every day.
How many beads do I eat in 2 days?

Our World

- Collect a range of small plastic creatures with legs, including people and birds. Ask the children to sort the creatures by the number of legs they have. Provide baskets or containers for the children to sort into and label each basket with the number of legs. Ask the children what they notice about the numbers. Discuss why legs come in pairs. Ask why there are no creatures with three or five legs. Can the children think of creatures with zero legs?

- Look under stones or bushes, or examine a spadeful of soil to find some minibeasts. Using a magnifying glass if necessary, sort the creatures into different trays according to the number of legs they have. Which tray has the most creatures in it? Are they all the same kind? Watch how the creatures move. Do all the legs on one side move together or do they move in pairs? Always return creatures to the wild after the session.

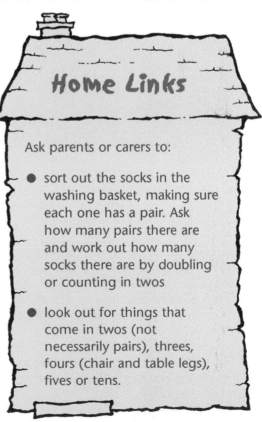

Home Links

Ask parents or carers to:

- sort out the socks in the washing basket, making sure each one has a pair. Ask how many pairs there are and work out how many socks there are by doubling or counting in twos

- look out for things that come in twos (not necessarily pairs), threes, fours (chair and table legs), fives or tens.

The Doorbell Rang

Learning Intentions

● To demonstrate an interest in number problems.

● To use developing mathematical knowledge to solve everyday problems.

● To begin to understand the concept of sharing.

● Ask the children how to share the cars if three children want to play. Check the children's understanding by repeating with a different toy a few days later.

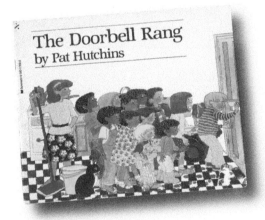

Starting Points

● Show the children a toy garage and six cars. Explain that two children want to play and ask them how they could make the game fair. Model sharing the cars by giving one car each to two children, then repeat until all the cars are used up.

● Read the story *The Doorbell Rang* by Pat Hutchins (published by Scholastic). Talk about what happened each time the doorbell rang. Emphasise that the characters share the cookies fairly between all the children.

Exploration

● Make a set of 12 cookies from salt dough. Provide two small baking trays and ask the children to put the cookies onto the trays so that there is the same number on each tray. If the group demonstrates a good understanding of sharing, produce an additional tray. Are they able to share the cookies fairly between three trays?

● Act out the story of *The Doorbell Rang* with children taking the parts of Ma, Victoria, Sam, Tom, Hannah, Peter, Peter's little brother, Joy, Simon and Grandma. Set a table with two plates and two cups. Provide a set of 12 salt-dough cookies and a further ten plates within easy reach. Use a bell for the doorbell.

● Focus on the need to share out the cookies again each time someone else arrives. Give the new arrivals a plate each and ask the children the best way to share out the cookies.

● Take photographs of the children to match the illustrations in the book. Use the photographs to make a class or group version of the book.

Free Play

● Set up a sharing table with bowls and counters, conkers or other small objects. Have only one set of objects out each day and make sure that the items are identical to ensure that sorting for colour or other attributes does not distract the children.

● Provide threading beads and laces. Ask the children to share the beads with a friend to make a necklace. Give a badge to children whose necklaces show that they shared with a friend.

Language and Literacy

- Invent more pages for the story of *The Doorbell Rang* – perhaps there could be three children initially to share 12 cookies. Add different characters and write out the new story on a white board.

- Discuss how Sam and Victoria felt each time the doorbell rang. Focus on the page where Ma advises the children to eat their cookies before she answers the door again. Ask the children if they think the characters' feelings were the same each time.

- Invite the children to make up their own sharing stories. With an adult acting as a scribe, make individual books illustrating the children's stories. A4 or A5 paper folded in half with a different colour used for the cover is ideal. Staple the book together after the pages have been illustrated.

Outside

- Provide a picnic basket and rug. Encourage the children to set the correct number of places and share pretend food fairly between each other or dolls.

- Whilst playing outside, talk to the children about sharing equipment. Ask for suggestions for sharing the larger equipment like the climbing frame and tricycles.

Creative

- Use circles of card as a base. Decorate with a range of materials such as coloured and shiny paper, wool and fabric to make amazing cookies.

- Set up a cookie stall. Tie or tape a long cane to each of the front legs of a table. Make a banner to attach to the top of the canes. Bake a range of salt-dough cookies, including geometric shapes. Dye the dough with food colouring or paint after baking. Sort and display the cookies for sale. Display with a price list and price labels. Provide paper bags and a till with plastic coins.

Our World

- Make real cookies to enjoy together. Look at how the mixture changes as the ingredients are combined, then how it has changed after cooking. Ask the children to share the mixture fairly between themselves so that everyone can make the same number of cookies.

Home Links

Ask parents or carers to:

- take their child to a market. Can they find a cookie stall, or one that sells cakes and biscuits? Look for labels showing ingredients as well as price

- collect cookie bags for the cookie stall.

- Make a cookie box. Turn a small box inside out by splitting it along the seam. Reverse all the folds and remake the box 'inside out'. Decorate the boxes using paints, recycled materials and sticky paper cookies. Line with tissue paper and add the baked cookies.

Let's Find Out

Learning Intentions

● To begin to make simple predictions and estimates.

● To begin to use developing mathematical understanding to solve simple puzzles and problems.

● To begin to suggest alternative ways of tackling a problem and to make decisions.

● To recognise, extend and create patterns.

Starting Points

● Show the children a large pile of coloured bricks. Discuss finding out which colour has the most bricks. Listen to the children's suggestions – for example, building a tower of each colour and then counting the total. Try each idea until a solution is found.

● Prepare some sticky number labels 0 to 10. Duplicate the numbers so that everyone is included. Stick a label on the back of each child's left hand. Tell the children to find a partner to make a specified total (for example, ten), or find a partner who is next on the number line, or find a partner with the same number.

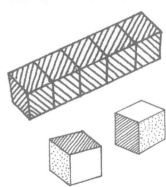

Exploration

● Explore the number six. Use an egg box and cubes of two colours. Count the number of spaces together. Invite each child to place a cube (of either colour) into each space. Count the cubes again to confirm that there are six in total. Create sums such as 'three red cubes and three green cubes make six altogether'. Repeat the activity with different colour formations.

● Find out more about the number six by taking some cubes away from a full egg box. Take two cubes away, saying 'six take away two leaves four'. Replace the cubes and repeat the activity by taking away different amounts.

- Use an inkpad to stamp identical pictures randomly onto a sheet of paper. Copy the sheets for everyone in the group. Show the children the sheet and count the pictures together. Ask the children to fold the paper so that they can see only three stamps. Encourage the children to find their own way after demonstrating other ways of folding the paper. Set several similar challenges.

- Provide a set of challenge cards such as: 'Build a tower as tall you'; 'Complete this jigsaw before the sand runs out in the timer'; 'How many cubes are there in this box?'; 'Find three children wearing stripes', and so on, as appropriate to the children.

- Ask an adult to wear a 'challenge apron'. Sew a large C on the front so that the adult is easily identified. Children could approach the adult to request a challenge, or the adult could ask a child if they would like a challenge. The 'challenge' adult could award a sticker when the challenge is completed.

Free Play

- Make some simple models from popular construction equipment. Photograph the models and laminate the pictures. List what is needed on the back of the photograph. Place a photograph and all the necessary pieces to make that particular model in a tray for the children to try.

- Provide games that require consideration of more than one attribute. A grid game with pictures of different shapes along the top row and splashes of different colours down the first column is ideal. Provide shapes or picture cards to be placed in the appropriate places on the grid.

Language and Literacy

- Tell a Maths story using props. Create a simple scene of a field with a river running through it from coloured paper. Build a bridge from interlocking bricks and collect a small group of play people.

- Explain that only one person can cross at a time. Count the people beside the river and then 'walk' them over the bridge, one at a time. Invite a different child to 'walk' each person across the bridge.

- Extend the story by asking each child to talk about the character as it goes across the bridge. As each person crosses, verbalise the sum, for example: 'Seven people waiting to cross, one has crossed, so that leaves six more to cross.'; 'Four people on this side, three people on that side, seven people altogether.'

Outside

- Design a Maths trail for the children. Try to use what is already there rather than making things specifically for the trail, for example the shape of the bricks in the wall, the number of drainpipes, measure the length of a bench with your hand, and so on. The trail could extend indoors too.

- Fill some trays with water. Provide a range of construction equipment. Challenge the children to build a bridge so that play people can cross the lake without getting wet. Make sure that none of the construction equipment has large enough pieces to span a tray with one piece.

Creative

- Provide a set of thick and thin paints, both with the same colours, and a range of different papers, including some unusual choices such as sandpaper and corrugated paper. Encourage the children to try both types of paint on any particular sheet of paper. Ask them which type of paint they prefer and why.

- Prepare some pre-cut shapes (triangles, squares, circles, and so on) in a small range of colours. Provide some strips of paper, wide enough for a single shape but long enough for several. Prepare a few examples of repeating patterns, including some with the same initial shapes. Encourage the children to make their own repeating pattern, using as many (or as few) different shapes and colours as they wish.

Our World

- Teach the children to count in another language. Begin with one, two and three, extending to ten later. Choose a language appropriate to some of the children, for example one that some children speak at home. Look at a map of the world and identify parts of the world where the language is spoken. Explain that if a class of children in that country were counting now, they would be counting in their own language.

- Make up some trays of damp sand and leave a clear imprint of something familiar to the children in the sand. Invite the children to look at the imprints but not touch them. Can they identify which items made the imprint in the sand? Have a 'check' tray where the children can check the imprint of the items they suggest.

Home Links

Ask parents or carers to:

- involve their child in supermarket shopping by asking questions such as 'Are there enough apples here for you to take one to school every day?'

- count with their child in the language the children have been practising. Point out items from that country in the supermarket or on television, and so on.

63

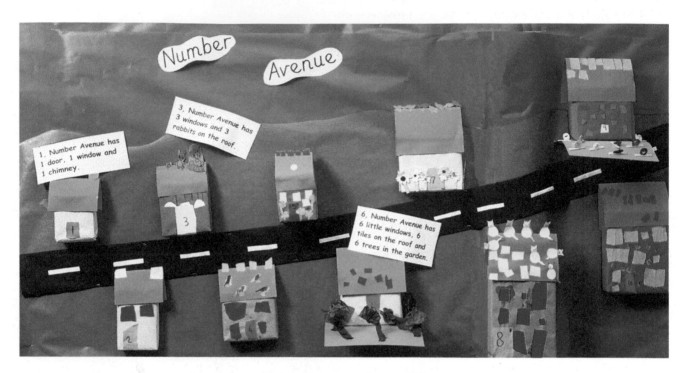

Number Avenue (page 13)